T0031673

Real Estate the Ramsey Way

By wisdom a house is built, and through
understanding it is established
Proverbs 24:3

Real Estate the Ramsey Way

Making Home Ownership a Blessing, Not a Burden

DAVE RAMSEY

RAMSEY
P R E S S

Editor: Kris Bearss
Cover Design: Chris Carrico and Weylon Smith
Photography: Seth Farmer
Interior Design: PerfecType Typesetting, Nashville, TN

ISBN: 979-8-887820-24-8

Printed in the United States of America
24 25 26 27 28 JST 5 4 3 2 1

Real Estate the Ramsey Way

Making Homeownership a Blessing, Not a Burden

One thing's for sure. If you've picked up this book, you've got the fever. *House fever.* That's the best reason I can think of to read a book about real estate anyway. You probably have other symptoms too. Maybe your heart races every time your phone buzzes with another Zillow notification. Or maybe you're an otherwise perfectly sane person who suddenly can't resist stalking your dream neighborhood in search of For Sale signs a couple times a week.

Or you could have the seller's version of house fever. House fever doesn't discriminate. It usually starts with a For Sale sign that pops up in your neighborhood, with you thinking to yourself, *I wonder how much they're asking?* You check out the listing . . . and your jaw hits the floor. If they could get *that much* for their house, how much could you get for yours? And just like that, your house is on the market—and you've got zero plans but lots of fever.

I get it. I've been on both sides of house fever a bazillion times in my life. Because I love real estate! I grew up in the real estate business.

My mom and dad owned a real estate company, and I learned the ins and outs from them. When I was 18, I took the real estate license exam in 27 minutes and scored 94 percent. (I imagine the test is harder now.) A couple of weeks later, I sold my first house. Imagine 18-year-old, just-out-of-high-school Dave in my disco clothes with a head full of hair, driving a two-door 1974 Monte Carlo. To this day, I'm shocked my first client didn't run the other way when I pulled up to their showing. Instead, they took a chance on that green-as-a-gourd, real estate rookie. And I'm so grateful they did!

In college, my dream was to become a real estate mogul. I got a finance degree with a specialization in real estate. And even though I knew practically nothing, I managed to convince people I did, and I sold real estate all through college—even while interest rates were topping out at 17 percent. So when I say I love real estate, I mean, I *really* love real estate.

That was more than 40 years ago. And my love and knowledge of real estate have only grown. But now what I love most is using the things I've learned to teach people like you how to buy and sell houses the right way. Because here's the thing: House fever can make us all stupid. It turns out buying or selling a house is an emotional process. And our emotions can make us lose focus, pay too much, or agree to a bad deal. Ultimately, house fever makes things messy. And that's the *last* thing you need when you're buying or selling the most expensive item you'll ever own.

How do I know? Bankruptcy, that's how—the toughest finance teacher of them all.

By age 26, I'd built a mini empire of more than $4 million in real estate, and I personally had a net worth of more than $1 million.

But I'd built the business with debt. And when my primary lender was sold to another bank, the new owners made the fateful decision to call all our notes . . . all at once. I spent the next three years losing everything I owned. I was sued so many times, my wife, Sharon, started making cookies for the sheriff's deputies who came to serve us with the papers. I was foreclosed on multiple times, and finally we went bankrupt.

Something happens to you when you can't pay your bills and your electricity gets cut off. When you don't know how you're going to buy food and provide for your wife, toddler, and new baby. You're not just broke, you're broken.

But when you're in the deepest valley, something else happens. You find hope in your faith, and your perspective about life and about yourself deepens. You choose to stand on your pile of mistakes instead of getting buried under it. You seek out knowledge and work to make better decisions with better information, to ultimately have more success. And all along, you strive to use your experience to help others be successful too.

That's my goal with this little book and the additional digital resources I'll point you to as we go. I've distilled my learnings from decades of making small-dollar and big-dollar real estate deals so you can apply them to your own buying, selling, and investing ventures. These simple principles are the same ones I've shared with thousands upon thousands of callers on *The Ramsey Show* to help them avoid the mistakes and pitfalls of what can be an otherwise ruthless business. Because real estate should be a blessing, not a burden—and not just for you. If you're doing it the right way, your buying, selling, and investing will become a generational blessing for your kids and grandkids . . . and *their* kids and grandkids. That's called a legacy. And you can start building yours right now.

Buying a Home: It's a Big Deal

For decades, I opened my radio show with the line: "Where the paid-off home mortgage has taken the place of the BMW as the status symbol of choice." And I meant it! In fact, a paid-for home is one of the keys to building wealth.

If you go into your home purchase thinking, *No one can afford to buy a house today and hope to pay it off in less than 30 years*, you're setting yourself up for financial disaster. It's true that your home is likely the largest purchase you'll ever make. It's also true that when you pay it off, your home will likely become your biggest asset.

That's why it's important to do this right! Folks call in to *The Ramsey Show* from all around the country who are buying homes the smart way, and yes—they're paying them off!

And the path they've followed starts with the 7 Baby Steps.

Follow the 7 Baby Steps

Before declaring bankruptcy, I paid off as much of the real estate debt as I could, and I destroyed my business to do it. But I still had a family to feed. And the bills and collections notices were still coming in. *Scared* doesn't begin to describe how I felt. I'd tried it my way, and my way didn't work. So I started reading everything I could get my hands on about how money really works. The principles I found weren't new. I stole them from God and your grandma. And they *did* work! They're the reason Sharon and I survived going broke and were able to rebuild.

The 7 Baby Steps grew out of those principles as well as thousands of conversations with real people on the radio, on TV, at live events, and at in-person financial counseling sessions. Today, millions of families have taken control of their money by following the Baby Steps. Those steps *are* the proven plan to win with money. They're the shortest distance between where you are now and lasting wealth. They show you how to live like no one else now, so you can live and give like no one else later. And we all need a path like that to run on.

The plan works every single time—but only when you follow each step in the right order:

1. Save $1,000 for your starter emergency fund.
2. Pay off all debt (except the house) using the Debt Snowball.
3. Save 3–6 months of expenses as a full emergency fund.
4. Invest 15 percent of your household income in retirement.
5. Save for your children's college fund.
6. Pay off your home early.
7. Build wealth and give.

So where does buying a house fit into this plan? After Steps 1–3. (There's another step in between Baby Steps 3 and 4 where you save for a down payment. I call it Baby Step 3b.) That's right. Don't go buying a house until you're 100 percent debt-free and have a full emergency fund as a safety net.

Does that sound crazy? I'll show you why it's not.

Don't Buy a House If You're in Debt

Our toxic money culture has convinced us that debt is a way of life. That you can't get by without debt and a "good" credit score. Spoiler alert: Yes, you can! The truth is, all debt creates risk—that's why debt is *dumb*. Not only that, but debt also cripples your ability to be a successful homeowner.

Take a look at the 7 Baby Steps again. If you're on Baby Step 2, that means you're chained to some sort of debt. It's weighing you down. Maybe it's credit card debt, student loans, car loans, personal loans, or a combination. That pile of debt robs you of your number-one wealth-building tool: your income. When most of your paycheck goes toward payments every month, you don't have any left over to save for emergencies, let alone to save a down payment for a house. And balancing those payments along with the costs of homeownership is a nightmare.

What if you already have a house and a mortgage and you're not debt-free? Should you sell the house to get out of debt? You could. But as I'll talk about later, selling isn't an easy fix. So, I'd only tell you to sell if the house is swallowing up too much of your household income each month.

Delay Your Daydream and Buy a House You Can Afford

Another big mistake I see first-time buyers make is believing they're entitled to the perfect dreamhouse they've always wanted, no matter how much it costs. They want their starter home to be the same quality as the house their parents worked their way up to own. But etch this in your brain: The number-one thing you're looking for is a home you can actually *afford*.

This goes back to what I said earlier about keeping your emotions in check. It really doesn't matter if you find a home with a fabulous kitchen or a huge backyard, and you have daydreams about the meals and memories you'll make there. If you can't pay the mortgage each month or find the cash to fix things when they break, you'll be what's known as *house poor*. Your home will own you, not the other way around. You need lots of margin—or breathing room—in your bank account to own a home *and* reach your other goals: things like putting money away for retirement, your kids' college, and home improvements.

The house for you is the house that fits your budget. And if you want to win financially, you may have to sacrifice the small things you want now so you can get the big things you want later. That's called delayed gratification. And it's what separates kids from adults. Children do what feels good. Adults devise a plan and follow it.

Okay, so how do you figure out how much house you can afford? We'll dig deeper into that later. But you can jump ahead and check out the resources we have on our website to answer that question by scanning this QR code.

Quick Answers to Common Real Estate Questions

Naturally, first-time homebuyers (and plenty of second- and third-time buyers) have a lot of questions. Questions like:

- What type of mortgage makes the most sense for my situation?
- What is title insurance—and do I really need it?
- What is PMI, and do I have to pay for that?
- How do I pay off my house sooner?
- What does it mean to have equity?
- What are property taxes?
- What is escrow—and do I need it?

Plus, the homebuying process has its own language, so there are lots of terms to learn as well. You can follow the QR code below to our FAQ webpage where I've answered these questions and provided definitions to common real estate terms all in one place.

Getting Ready to Buy

In September of 2019, Sarah and Justin came to our headquarters to share their debt-free story on *The Ramsey Show*. Incredibly, they'd paid off $185,000! When I asked how they planned to celebrate all their hard work, Sarah replied, "Oh, we're getting Baby Step 3b completed!"

Can you believe that? They'd spent five years scratching and clawing their way out of a $185,000 pit—and their plan was to keep right on scratching and clawing to save up for a home!

They'd been dreaming of buying a home for five years—ever since they got married. But because of their local real estate market, they knew they'd have to save at least six figures to have a 10–20 percent down payment for a home. Plus, they'd had $185,000 in debt standing in their way. It all seemed crazy and far away. But they were committed.

As Sarah and Justin worked the Baby Steps to pay off their debt, they learned to be disciplined. They budgeted and sacrificed. Their focused intensity helped them pay off their mountain of debt. And that gave them unstoppable momentum.

For three years after they were debt-free, they kept at it. Their goal: to host Thanksgiving 2022 in their first home. Sarah got a side gig. Justin brought in extra cash selling his retro shoes. They said no to a cruise and other trips with friends. Their motto was "Every little bit helps."

Since they didn't have any debt, they saved up their down payment faster than they imagined. By March 2022, they'd closed on their first home (with a 15 percent-plus down payment). And, yes, they hosted both their families for Thanksgiving that year. My guess is they'll host many more.

When you see houses listed for hundreds of thousands of dollars, it's easy to feel like you'll never save enough money to buy one of your own. But remember, the way to eat an elephant is one bite at a time. You save up for your down payment one paycheck at a time. It takes time, and that doesn't sound exciting. But believe me—the real excitement kicks in when you and your family are in your home, and you can actually enjoy all the things you've been dreaming about.

Sarah told me it wasn't easy going against the norm. Society, friends, and family constantly told them they just needed to buy a house already—that's what you do when you get married. But she and Justin have no regrets about waiting. "If we'd done the 'normal thing,' the house would have been a nightmare instead of a dream . . . because we wouldn't have been able to afford it or put anything in it," she said. "Delayed gratification is loving your future self even more. Our house is a dream that took eight years to come true."

How to Save a Down Payment the Smart Way

So how do you start saving your down payment? First you need a goal. Ideally, you want to put down at least 20 percent of your home's purchase price. Why? Putting down 20 percent means you don't have to pay for private mortgage insurance (PMI), which is a type of insurance that protects your lender if you stop making your mortgage payments. It makes your monthly mortgage payment more expensive, and it doesn't benefit you at all.

If you're a first-time homebuyer, a 5–10 percent down payment is okay too. Just be ready to pay that PMI—usually around 1 percent of your mortgage amount per year. No matter what, make sure your mortgage payment is no more than 25 percent of your monthly take-home pay on a 15-year fixed-rate mortgage. And stay away from expensive VA and FHA loans! (Don't worry, we'll cover more details on mortgage types in a later section.)

Sure, 5–20 percent of a home feels like a crazy amount of money to save. But it is possible! Suppose you're buying a $200,000 house or condo and want to save a $10,000–$40,000 down payment. If you tighten up your budget and stash away $1,000 of your monthly income, you could have that down payment saved in as little as 10 months, or just under four years if you go for the full 20 percent—not bad! And remember, you're debt-free when you're doing this. All that money you were throwing at your debt and then your emergency fund can now go straight to your down payment savings. That makes setting aside $1,000 a month seem a lot more doable, doesn't it?

But what does it look like in real life? You'll save up your down payment faster with these five key principles:

1. **Follow a budget.** A budget is the best way to control your money. When you make your budget, your first priority after you cover the essentials is your monthly down payment savings goal. If you've never set up a budget, our free budgeting app, EveryDollar, will walk you through the steps.

2. **Tighten your spending (temporarily).** Once your budget is nailed down, cut any unnecessary spending. Postpone fancy vacations, eat out less, and suspend subscriptions (bye-bye, Netflix) so you can pile up more cash for your down payment.

3. **Use a money market savings account.** Keep your down payment savings in a safe place that's easy for you to access—like a simple money market savings account. No, you won't make tons on interest, but this isn't an investment. Especially if you plan to use the money in five years or less.

4. **Hold off on your retirement savings (temporarily).** Pause your contributions to your retirement accounts (even the match) while you save up your down payment. And get it saved as fast as possible so you can get back to building wealth for retirement.

5. **Start a side hustle.** To really hit the gas on your down payment savings, pick up a side job. Nothing fancy—you won't work there forever. Deliver some pizzas, drive for Uber, or try a freelance gig.

Know How Much House You Can Afford

You'll need a realistic goal for your down payment. And that starts with knowing how much house you can afford. I've talked with too many people who mess this up. They make a home purchase that's way over their heads and start drowning in mortgage payments. And that usually leads to foreclosure. I don't want the bank to repossess your house. I want your house to be a blessing that builds wealth for your family for generations to come. So, let's get you into a house you can actually afford from the start.

The simple key to knowing how much house you can afford is to make sure your mortgage payments are no more than 25 percent of your monthly take-home pay on a 15-year fixed-rate mortgage. Take-home pay is also called *net income*—the amount that goes into your bank account after taxes. If you're married, include your spouse's net monthly income in this amount.

And that 25 percent limit includes everything—principal, interest, property taxes, home insurance, and—depending on your situation—homeowners association (HOA) fees and PMI. (I'll cover what all of those mean a little later.)

Once you figure out how much your monthly take-home pay is, just multiply that number by 25 percent to get your max monthly house payment. If you take home $6,600 a month, for example, your monthly house payment should be no more than $1,650.

Use our mortgage calculator tool with the QR code below to help you calculate your mortgage amount, down payment, and monthly payment.

Don't Rush to Buy

Let's talk about renting for a minute.

Hear me when I say that renting is not a waste of money. It's not just paying someone else's mortgage. In fact, renting could be the absolute right move to make, depending on your situation. You should rent if you're:

- new to an area and don't yet know what part of town is for you.
- engaged (each of you need to rent your own place) or newly married.
- still in debt or don't have an emergency fund.
- in a transitional period of life, like you just graduated from college or you're getting started in your career and need the flexibility to move quickly.

Despite what you'll hear from pretty much anyone else in your life, renting does have benefits—if you do it right. First of all, you don't have to live in a luxury apartment. If you're working hard to pay off debt or save your down payment, keep your rent as low as possible. Get roommates or move to a cheaper place for a while.

Second, a history of on-time rent payments will help you buy a house if you don't have a credit score (which is possible since you'll stop using credit and pay off your debt before you buy a home).

Renting also means you don't have to pay for all the expenses that go along with homeownership. Homeowners have to be ready to pay for things like lawn equipment, landscaping, replacing broken or outdated appliances, and general upkeep. You're not ready to buy until you have room in your budget for those costs as well as the margin to save for really big home-maintenance projects like replacing your roof or resurfacing your driveway.

To help you make sure you're in the right shape to buy, my team built a free online assessment. Follow the QR code to take our "Am I Ready to Buy a Home?" quiz.

Find the Best Real Estate Agent

After you've piled up enough cash for your down payment, you're ready for the next step: finding a real estate agent. Yes, the confessed real estate junkie is telling you to work with a real estate agent. Because here's the deal: The real estate realm comes with lots of unknowns—pitfalls that can snag you and your money. So don't do this alone. Nothing compares to the ongoing support of a local expert who eats, sleeps, and breathes real estate. And that's true when you sell your home too. You need an experienced real estate veteran who does this stuff every single day.

Here is what you can expect from a great buyer's agent:

- **Helps you find the right house.** Your local agent is your insider connection. They can get you the latest updates on homes in your price range—sometimes before a home hits the market. They'll also set up home showings that work with your schedule.

- **Guides you on the offer and negotiations.** The best agents are expert negotiators. They know what similar houses are selling for in your area, so they won't let you lowball an offer so much that you miss out on a great buy—but they won't let you overpay either.
- **Walks you through the paperwork.** A home purchase creates a mountain of paperwork. Your agent will help you stay organized and on time, making sure all your i's are dotted and your t's are crossed.
- **Advises you on the home inspection.** Your agent can guide you on what to do if the inspection uncovers serious flaws with the home you want to buy.
- **Calms your nerves when things get tough.** Whether it's a problem with the appraisal or a hitch in your financing, a great agent knows how to keep things moving smoothly.

How to Choose the Right Agent

You probably already know some real estate agents in your area. But they don't all bring the same knowledge and experience to the table. Set the bar high and work with a true professional! Here's the kind of agent you're looking for:

- Ranks in the top 10 percent of agents in the market they serve. In other words, they do more deals on average and will bring more expertise to help you buy (or sell) a house compared to the other 90 percent of the competing agents in their market.

- Serves both buyers and sellers in all types of markets.
- Maintains a super-serving attitude that makes you feel like you're their only client.
- Responds quickly and consistently to your calls or emails.
- Provides references so you can find out how they treated past clients.
- Shares your financial values and won't pressure you into buying a house you can't afford.
- Has the heart of a teacher.

Don't make the mistake of hiring the first agent you talk to just to save time! Interview at least three agents before you make a decision. You can separate the pros from the duds with the right questions, like:

- How long have you been a full-time agent in my market?
- How many homes do you close on per year?
- How will you help me buy a home in this market?
- How will you communicate with me, and who will be my primary contact?
- What sets you apart from other real estate agents?
- What's your commission fee?
- Do I have to sign a contract with you, and can I cancel without penalty?
- Who can I contact for a reference? (Be sure that previous clients are on this list.)
- How do you set realistic expectations for your clients?

If you have a friend who's a real estate agent, proceed with caution. Interview them just like you would any other agent. And if they don't measure up, don't work with them. Never work with someone just because they're a friend.

My team searches for real estate agents across the country to find the ones who meet the qualifications above. Excellent, experienced agents who actually care about your budget and financial goals are the only kind of agents we trust to help you buy or sell a house—that's why we call them RamseyTrusted. So if you want a quick and easy way to find RamseyTrusted agents in your local area, use the following QR code.

How Much Does a Buyer's Agent Cost?

In most states, working with a real estate agent is free for buyers. Normally, the seller covers the commission for your buyer's agent. That means there's no reason to try and do this on your own. Your buyer's agent represents you and your best interests. They'll put their negotiation skills to work to get you the best price and the sweetest deal.

Get Preapproved for a Mortgage

Until now, your homebuying journey has been between you, your spouse if you're married, and your real estate agent. Now it's time to get a lender involved. Before you go house hunting, get a preapproval letter from your mortgage lender. This is different than getting prequalified. A lender can prequalify you to buy a house after a quick conversation about your income, assets, and down payment. But getting preapproved will take a little more work—and it's worth it!

For a preapproval, your lender will verify your financial information and submit your loan for preliminary underwriting. In a seller's eyes, that extra step puts your offer ahead of competing offers that are only prequalified.

Also, since your information is already in the lender's system, being preapproved can speed up the loan process once the seller accepts your offer—which definitely helps in a competitive market.

Credit Scores

If you ask just about any lender what it takes to get approved for a mortgage, they'll say you need a credit score in the mid-600s or higher. But here's a secret the toxic money culture doesn't want you to know: You don't even need a credit score to buy a house (*Gasp!*). If you've been living a debt-free lifestyle, you probably don't have a credit score—and that's a great thing!

All you have to do is work with a lender that does *manual under-writing*. This is when a lender personally reviews your payment records, income, and savings to make sure you're in good shape to take on a mortgage. If you can show that you pay your bills and you're following the guidelines we've laid out here (a good down payment on a 15-year mortgage with a payment that's no more than 25 percent of your take-home pay), you shouldn't have any trouble getting approved for a loan through manual underwriting.

One more thing about credit scores: *No* credit isn't the same as *bad* credit. Buying a house with bad credit is a terrible idea. If your credit score is lower than the mid-600 range, you'll only be eligible for crappy, high-interest loans. If you have bad credit, cut up your credit cards and cancel the accounts. Then go back to the Baby Steps and focus on paying off all your debt before buying a house. It's the only way to do it right.

Understand Your Mortgage Payment

Joseph and Bethany started their marriage in a one-bedroom apartment. After a year, they upgraded to a two-bedroom. And two years after that, they decided they were ready to buy their first house.

They'd had no trouble making their monthly rent payment or paying for renter's insurance. How different could it be to step up to a house payment, right? Well, as they were signing the papers to close on their home, they found out that a lot more goes into a monthly house payment than they imagined.

Of course, they'd already planned for the monthly principal and interest payment on their mortgage. But then there was the escrow to cover property taxes and homeowner's insurance. And then, because they were only able to put 10 percent down, they got hit with a $266 PMI fee each month on top of everything else.

Even though they felt blindsided by a much larger payment than they originally planned for, they were able to make it work. But that doesn't have to happen to you. Let's talk about what will go into your monthly mortgage payment:

- **Principal.** This is the portion of your payment that goes toward the original amount of money you borrowed to buy your house.
- **Interest.** Lenders make money on loans by charging a fee called *interest*—calculated as a percentage of the principal. Side note: If you're following the Ramsey way of doing real estate, don't let high interest rates scare you out of buying a house. You can always refinance your mortgage later to get a better rate.
- **Property taxes.** Local governments raise money through property taxes to fund things like schools, law enforcement, fire departments, and (supposedly) fixing potholes.
- **Home insurance.** Your mortgage lender will require you to have homeowner's coverage, and that will add a few more dollar signs to your house payment. But it'll literally pay off if your house is damaged or destroyed.

- **Private mortgage insurance.** As I mentioned, PMI is a fee that gets added to your mortgage payment if your down payment is less than 20 percent. It protects your lender (not you) from losing money if you stop making payments on your loan.

Many homeowners find it easiest to pay all these costs in one monthly payment. The principal and interest portion of your payment gets applied to your loan. And the part of your payment that goes toward taxes and insurance goes into an escrow account. When it's time to pay the insurance premium and property tax bill, your lender pays those bills on your behalf from escrow. Keep in mind that your mortgage payments may go up from year to year if there's a property tax hike or your insurance premiums increase. The escrow account is usually optional, but without it, you'll be responsible for making those payments in full when they're due.

In addition to all those costs, you might also have to pay a monthly homeowner's association (HOA) fee that helps to cover community maintenance and upgrades. If you buy a house in a community with an HOA, you automatically become a member and will be expected to pay the fee and keep your home up to HOA standards. The idea is these standards help maintain property values for homes in that community.

Remember, if your total monthly house payment is more than 25 percent of your take-home pay, consider it a red flag that you're just not ready to buy a house yet—or you need to find a cheaper house or save a bigger down payment to make the numbers work.

Know the Types of Mortgages

When we went through bankruptcy, Sharon and I decided we'd never borrow money again. And we haven't—not even for a mortgage. But most folks don't want to wait until they can pay cash to buy a home. Since your home will increase in value over time (adding to your net worth, by the way), a mortgage is the one kind of debt I won't yell at you about—as long as you do it right. And like we've talked about already, the only type of mortgage I ever recommend is a 15-year fixed-rate conventional mortgage. Here's why:

1. **Helps you get out of debt faster.** Most people take out a 30-year mortgage when they buy a home. But a 15-year mortgage means you'll own your home in half the time (ideally, less than that!).
2. **Protects you from rising interest rates.** A fixed-rate loan means your interest rate stays the same for the life of the loan. You'll never have to worry about paying a higher interest rate on your mortgage than when you first took it out.
3. **Saves you thousands (even hundreds of thousands) of dollars in interest fees.** With a 15-year mortgage, your monthly payment is larger than it would be on a 30-year loan, but that means more of your money goes to pay off the principal balance rather than going toward interest.

The savings really is the biggest reason to choose a 15-year loan. Let's look at the comparison on a $300,000 mortgage:

- You'll put down 20 percent, so the total loan amount is $240,000.
- You'll get a better interest rate on a 15-year fixed-rate loan. We'll say 3.5 percent, versus 4 percent on a 30-year loan.
- The payment on the 15-year loan is $600 more than the payment on the 30-year loan. But it all goes to pay down the principal.
- At the end of the loan, you'll have paid a total of $309,000 on the 15-year mortgage ($69,000 in interest), but $412,000 on the 30-year mortgage ($172,000 in interest).
- You'd pay over $100,000 *more* to borrow the same amount of money. Don't do it!

Now, what's the big deal about a conventional loan? A conventional loan isn't insured or guaranteed by the government; it's backed by private lenders. In 2022, 76 percent of new-home sales were financed with conventional loans, 9 percent were FHA loans, 5 percent were VA loans, and 10 percent were bought with cash.[1]

Conventional loans can be more flexible, but they can also be harder for buyers to qualify for. That's because, without government backing, conventional loans are riskier for lenders. But those extra hoops lenders make you jump through (like requiring a down payment) actually help protect you financially.

---

1. Statista Research Department, "Number of new home sales in the U.S. 2000-2022, by financing type," statista.com (February 10, 2023), https://www.statista.com/statistics/185206/us-house-sales-with-fha-and-va-insured-mortgages-from-2002/.

Bottom line: A government loan will cost you more in the long run. Stay far away!

Avoid These Rip-Off Mortgages

While we're at it, let's talk about *all* the mortgage types to steer clear of. Anything other than a 15-year fixed-rate conventional loan will drown you in interest and fees and keep you in debt for decades. But that won't stop your lender from offering up bad loan options. Just say *no thanks* to these rip-off mortgages:

- **30-year conventional.** Lower payments can make a 30-year mortgage attractive. But the interest rate will be higher (compared to a 15-year), and you have to make payments for decades. A lot of people get the 30-year loan and say they'll pay extra on it, but there's always something else to spend your money on. Don't fall for it.
- **ARM (adjustable-rate mortgage).** This option offers a lower interest rate (and monthly payment) for the first few years. But an ARM transfers the risk of rising interest rates from the lender to you. When the rate increases, your payment can quickly become too much for you to afford.
- **FHA loan (Federal Housing Administration).** Sure, an FHA loan will allow you to buy a house with a down payment as little as 3.5 percent. But in exchange, you'll be charged an extra fee for the life of the loan—on top of all the

extra interest you'll pay and the decades you'll spend in debt for not making a bigger down payment. Bad idea.

- **VA loan (US Department of Veterans Affairs).** A VA loan helps veterans get into a house with no money at all. But when you purchase a home with zero money down, you pay way more in interest—plus the funding fees that come with a VA loan. No thanks.

- **USDA loan (US Department of Agriculture).** A USDA loan is designed to help people in rural areas who can't really afford to buy a home yet, get into a house with zero money down. But again, all the added interest payments will crush your budget over the years! Plus, if you can't afford to put any money down on a house, you're not ready to handle the maintenance and other costs that come with homeownership.

Choosing the Right House

After you're preapproved for a mortgage, you're ready for the fun part: house hunting! You (and your spouse if you're married) need to make a list of must-haves for your home. This list does two things: (1) It gets you and your spouse on the same page about which features or amenities are really important in your first home; and (2) you can share your list with your real estate agent to help them target the kind of home you're looking for.

Be careful not to confuse things you need with things you want. Sure, it'd be nice to have a house in a gated community with upscale finishes and perfect color combos. But there's also nothing wrong with a home with good bones that needs a little work. Some buyers can't see past easy-to-fix details like décor and paint color—and that could score *you* a deal!

Remember, this is your first home. Not your dream home. Be honest about what you can afford. You may need to reset your expectations about size, features, and how move-in ready the home will be.

And don't forget—location, location, location! Aim to buy the smallest (or even the worst) house in the nicest neighborhood you can afford. Even if you believe you're buying your forever home, keep resale value in mind. Pay attention to what's happening in the community where you're looking to buy. Are home values rising or declining? Are businesses booming or closing? Will the area be attractive to buyers several years down the road? If new homes are being built in the area, that's a good sign growth will continue.

Making the Offer

When you get to the offer stage, you've got to work hard to keep your emotions in check. You may have waited years to get to this point—and now's not the time to get carried away. Lean on your agent's knowledge and experience as you put together an offer that's based on facts, not your feelings.

A fact-based offer starts with the comparative market analysis (CMA, or comps) your agent provides you that shows listings and sale prices for homes in the neighborhood where you're planning to buy. If those comparable homes are selling for 5 percent less on average than their listing prices, you can reasonably offer 8–10 percent less than the listing price and leave yourself room to negotiate. See? Facts are your friends!

Of course, the approach you take depends on the market in your area. If it's really slow, you might score a deal by making a low offer. But if it's a seller's market, other hungry buyers could quickly outbid you. An experienced agent can tell you the best route to take. But no matter what, make sure you're comfortable with your offer. After all, it's *your* money on the line!

Once you've settled on a price, your agent will help you fill out a sales and purchase agreement, a legal document that covers all the terms and conditions of your offer along with important details such as:

- Buyer and seller information
- Proposed closing date
- Purchase price, lender information, and down payment amount
- Earnest money amount (this is sort of like a security deposit that can also be used toward your down payment or closing costs)
- Items you want left with the home (appliances or furniture)
- Contingencies (like home inspection, appraisal, and final mortgage approval)

Once your agent sends the agreement to the seller's agent, you wait. Sometimes agreeing on terms is quick and painless. But it can also be one of the most difficult parts of the process. If you end up in a bidding war with other buyers, don't panic. Keep a cool head and put your best foot forward. Being preapproved with your lender and having a flexible closing date can give you a leg up on the competition, especially for a seller looking for a quick sale.

But never offer more than you can afford—even if the lender says you're approved for more. No house is worth being house poor.

Negotiating the Deal

It'd be awesome to turn in an offer, have the seller accept it word for word, then live happily ever after. But that rarely happens. Welcome to the negotiation phase.

Sellers usually come back with a counteroffer that changes or adds to the terms you offered. A seller may have their own contingencies, like a delay on the closing date until they find a new home. Or they might want a kick-out clause that allows them to keep the home listed—meaning your offer could be kicked out if they get a better offer.

Your agent should explain how the counteroffer affects you and also help you make a counteroffer of your own if that's the step you decide to take. If you're a cash buyer, or you've been preapproved (not just prequalified) for a mortgage, or you don't have to sell your current house before you buy, you likely have the upper hand in the negotiations.

Keep in mind, there's much more to negotiating than simply wrestling over the price. As a buyer, you can negotiate anything. All you have to do is ask! Sellers are often eager to seal the deal, so you might be surprised by what they'll agree to.

In exchange for paying their full asking price, you could ask the seller to throw in a washer and dryer for example. Do you see something that needs fixed or replaced? Ask them to pay for repairs. Anything from a new paint job to furniture is fair game. Use your imagination!

If things get intense, remember that both you and the seller want the same thing: They want to sell their home, and you want to buy it. Sometimes it pays to compromise on the small stuff to keep moving forward. A good real estate agent can give you advice about when to give in and when to stand firm.

Always Get a Home Inspection

One thing that should never be on the negotiation table, however, is the home inspection. The point of a home inspection is to uncover any major problems like structural issues or expensive repairs. If anything like that turns up, you can ask the seller to fix the problem, reduce the price, or cancel the contract.

A home inspection costs a few hundred dollars. As the buyer, you choose your inspector and pay for the inspection shortly after the seller accepts your offer. Your agent may suggest a few home inspectors you can talk to, or you can search online and find plenty of licensed inspectors. If you're buying an older home or a home that needs work, also ask your agent about getting other professional evaluations such as a radon test or a termite inspection.

When you're getting a home loan, your lender will require an appraisal (which you'll also pay for) to make sure the price you're paying is fair for the type of house you're buying in that local market. If the appraisal comes in lower than your offer price, that doesn't always mean the deal is down the drain. But you do have some decisions to make. Your real estate agent will help you sort through your options.

Walk-Away Power

Here's the important thing to remember about negotiations: Predators can sense fear in their prey. And sellers can sense when you're desperate to buy their house—and they'll often take advantage of it.

You can eliminate that advantage by being prepared to walk away from a deal. Until both sides sign the agreement, either party can reject the offer and end all negotiations. Sometimes it's just a bluff, but other times it's best to walk away and live to buy another day— without regrets!

Final Mortgage Approval

After you and the seller reach an agreement, your lender will dig into your finances to finalize your mortgage. This usually takes around 30 days but can take up to 60 days or more in some circumstances. Whatever you do, don't open a new credit account, take on more debt, or change jobs once you're under contract. Taking on debt is a bad idea anytime, but any changes to your income or overall financial situation can jeopardize your loan approval.

During this time, make sure you're ready for the additional costs leading up to, and on, closing day. On average, buyers pay 3–4 percent of a home's purchase price for closing costs, depending on your market and the type of loan you're getting. This includes expenses like loan origination fees, credit reports, underwriting fees, appraisal fees, and title fees. Note: Your lender will require you to have home insurance before your mortgage can be finalized. Since your insurance premium and property taxes fall in the category of prepaids, you'll pay your premium and property taxes for the remainder of the year at closing as well.

Your lender is required to give you a Closing Disclosure at least three days before your closing date. It will list out all the details about who pays what at closing. You'll pay any of the costs you're responsible for with a cashier's check or wire transfer.

Some lenders allow you to roll all those costs into your mortgage, but don't sign up for that. Why? Because you'll pay interest on those costs for the life of your loan, and that'll amount to way more of your hard-earned money spent.

Believe You Can Pay Off Your House

Congratulations! You're a homeowner! You got into your home the right way. Now it's time to get *out* of that mortgage.

Pay it off as fast as you can! When you do real estate the Ramsey way, you set yourself up to live like nobody else. You'll be debt-free, living in a paid-for house and using your income to build wealth and give generously. Anytime you feel like it's too much or it's taking too long, remember Eddie and Marney's story.

In 2014, Eddie came across my show while scanning through radio stations at work one day. He heard a couple tell the story of how they became debt-free. Then Eddie heard me say, "Count it down and let's hear your Debt-Free Scream!" When the couple shouted at the top of their lungs, "Weeeee're debt-*freeeeeee!*" Eddie had a visceral, emotional response. He wanted that freedom for himself and for his wife, Marney.

He told Marney about what he'd heard and got her listening to the show too. That's all it took to get her on board. Over the next six years, they tackled their debt as a team. They saved up their fully funded emergency fund. But they didn't stop there.

One day, not long after they'd paid off their debt, Eddie was standing in their backyard looking at their brand-new storage shed. "The shed was paid in full. I owned it," Eddie said. But it dawned on him that while the shed was paid for, the house wasn't. "If we were to lose the house," he said, "we would lose the shed too."

After that, he and Marney got serious about paying off their house. They made extra principal payments with every paycheck. "We were slowly watching the total come down," Marney said. "I told my husband I felt like we were a couple of devouring locusts. I also had a mantra: *Plan our attack and attack our plan!*"

As they closed in on that zero mortgage balance, Marney started posting about their progress in our Facebook community. When she and Eddie got down to less than $10,000, you could feel the excitement in the comments on their posts. So many people—people they didn't even know—were cheering them on to the final payment!

They paid off $70,400 in 23 months! And in February 2023, Eddie and Marney were officially free from their mortgage. In fact, they paid it off on February 3 so their payoff date would be memorable: 2-3-23. They're still adjusting to not having a mortgage payment. "It feels like we're living someone else's story," Marney said. "I'm just in awe of where we are financially."

People like Eddie and Marney are weird! And I love it! It's completely countercultural to not have any debt—not even a house payment. That's why you buy a home the Ramsey way: so that one day (sooner than you think) your home will belong totally to you. You don't owe anything to anyone. It's a great feeling! Even the grass under your feet feels different when you own your home.

Don't believe me? There's only one way to find out.

Selling Your Home: It's a Big Deal Too!

For more than 15 years, Darren and Kenya lived just outside of Chicago. They were leading a super-busy life keeping up with their four increasingly active kids. "We have a competitive swimmer, a competitive figure skater, a competitive hockey player, and a rugby player," Kenya said. Their kids' busy schedules were starting to be a strain on the family—but that's not all they were dealing with. Add in their ongoing money problems, Darren's high-stress job, and aging parents with health issues, and you can understand why Darren and Kenya felt like they were drowning in their lives. It was time to make a change. They decided to leave Illinois and start a new life near their parents in Florida.

Just one problem (on top of all the others): They'd need to sell their house.

On one hand, Darren and Kenya knew their home sale could be a game changer for them. Their home was valued at around $176,000, and they had a ton of equity—over $145,000. That would give them more than enough to pay off their remaining debt and cover the cost of their move.

On the other hand, they knew their house needed a lot of work. "We had bought it as a fixer-upper," Kenya said. "But it needed a new roof and new carpet, the kitchen and deck needed to be updated, and the water softener was broken and leaking. We also had a leak in the upstairs bathroom that dripped into the downstairs bathroom."

Next came the news that Darren had landed a job in Jacksonville. His start date was just a month away! Was that a blessing? Yes! But it also threw another challenge into the mix: They only had one month to sell the house and move a family of six! As first-time sellers, Darren and Kenya knew they were getting in way over their heads. So they started looking for a real estate agent to help them navigate it all.

The first agent they talked to took a look at all the work that needed to be done and suggested they spend $20,000–$25,000 on the house just to make it ready to sell. The upside, according to the agent, was that those improvements would allow them to list their house for $190,000–$200,000. The agent completely ignored the fact that Darren and Kenya didn't have that kind of money or the time to get the work completed. Bottom line: It was a bad plan that benefited the agent, not Darren and Kenya.

"The last thing we could afford was an agent who was just concerned about their own paycheck," Darren said.

The next one they talked to was a RamseyTrusted real estate agent. And the experience was completely different. Their new agent looked the house over but spent most of her time talking with Darren and Kenya about their goals and listening as they explained their financial challenges and stressful schedule. The agent told them to price the house low and sell it as is.

"That was the most wonderful thing about her," Kenya said. "She understood our situation."

"She didn't give us any false expectations," Darren added. "She gave us hope without getting our hopes up too high—and she gave us confidence to know that we could do it. I know our real estate agent had a lot of other customers with houses more valuable than ours, but it felt like we were her only customers."

As soon as Darren and Kenya took care of some basic cleaning and decluttering, their real estate agent listed the house for $167,000. She even gave them six movie tickets so the whole family could get away together during the open house. That weekend, they had a whirlwind of home showings, and by Tuesday, they had three offers! By the end of the week, they had a signed contract for a sale price of $177,000!

Just as they hoped, the profits of the sale were more than enough to pay off their mortgage and cover their closing costs and agent commissions. Everything else went into their savings. "We will definitely be able to put 20 percent down for our next house and pay cash for a nice used car," Kenya said.

"It's never too late to do the right thing or to ask for help," Darren said. "We were in a pretty bad spot, and I'm thankful that it was easy to find a RamseyTrusted real estate agent in our area."

Always Sell with a Top Agent

Selling your home is just as big a deal as buying it—it's one of the most expensive things you'll ever own. And you invest a lot of your time, money, and emotion in your home. So when it comes time to sell, you want to get it right. That's why I'll always tell you to work with an experienced real estate agent to sell your home, just like I do for folks looking to buy a home.

If you skipped over the homebuying section, go back and take a look at the guidelines for choosing a real estate agent (pages XX-XX). Remember, you're looking for excellence. That means you want a solid communicator, a coach who can explain the process, a confidence-booster, and someone who's a top closer in your market.

You can find those real estate rockstars by asking good questions (and knowing the answers to listen for). Just scan the QR code below to find our free Real Estate Agent Interview Worksheet. And don't forget, you can also use the QR code to find agents we recommend in your area through our RamseyTrusted program.

Why Not Sell It Yourself?

Just like with homebuying, I see a lot of people make big mistakes when they decide to sell their home. One of the biggest is trying to sell your home yourself to save on the commission. After all, the argument goes, the standard commission for a real estate transaction is 6 percent of the property's sale price divided up between the seller's agent and the buyer's agent. And since the seller usually covers the commission for both agents, that's a big chunk of money coming out of your proceeds.

Let me stop you right there. Selling your home yourself, or doing For Sale by Owner (FSBO—as it's known in the real estate biz), is a great way to lose a lot of money. The truth is, a good real estate agent will make you more money than they cost you in commissions. Now, I've learned that people are going to do what they're going to do. If you're dead set on selling your home yourself, I'm not going to convince you not to. But if you truly want to know why FSBO is such a bad idea, I've got three good reasons:

1. **Lower profit.** Every year, data shows how FSBO homes sell for thousands (even hundreds of thousands) of dollars less than agent-assisted homes. According to a National Association of REALTORS® (NAR) study covering a recent 12-month period, home sellers who went the FSBO route sold their homes at a median price of $225,000, compared to those who sold with a real estate agent at $345,000.[2] That's

---

2. National Association of REALTORS®, "Highlights From the Profile of Home Buyers and Sellers," nar.realtor (November 2023), https://

a $120,000 difference! You don't have to be a genius at math to see that's more than enough to cover the commission.

Really good agents know how to help you sell your home for more money than you could get selling solo. Plus, selling FSBO doesn't guarantee you won't end up paying the buyer's agent commission. So why try to sell without an expert on *your* side?

2. **Limited exposure.** To sell your home, you need buyer leads—and lots of them! An experienced real estate agent has the connections you need to get those leads. Your online FSBO post just can't compete.

3. **Unintentional mishaps.** Even though I've bought and sold real estate for decades, I know not to take unnecessary risks with my largest asset. And you shouldn't either. An expert agent probably sold more homes last week than you've sold in a lifetime. That means they know how to avoid even the small mistakes that can cost you big. They've seen it all before and can navigate through pitfalls and paperwork you never saw coming. That kind of expertise is worth its weight in gold.

The downside to FSBO is no secret to most sellers. Only a very small percentage of sellers, about 1 in 10, even choose to sell solo.[3] Don't make that mistake.

---

www.nar.realtor/research-and-statistics/research-reports/highlights-from -the-profile-of-home-buyers-and-sellers/.

3. "Highlights From the Profile of Home Buyers and Sellers."

Make Sure You're Ready to Sell

Anytime the housing market heats up, you'll see all kinds of people coming down with house fever. After all, if homes near you are selling like hotcakes—and for top dollar—maybe yours will too! But market conditions don't dictate the right time to sell your home. Only your personal situation and finances do that. Here's how to decide if you're ready to sell:

- **You're debt-free with an emergency fund.** You guessed it, the same rules apply to buyers *and* sellers. Dump your debt and get your emergency fund in the bank before you enter the real estate ring. That way you're in a good position financially to buy your next home.
- **You can afford the costs.** First, set aside enough money for staging, closing costs, and moving expenses. Next, consider the cost of your next home compared to the profit you expect to make on the sale of your current home. Could you pay for your new home in cash? At the very least, you need to clear enough to make a 20 percent down payment on your next home. Stick to a 15-year fixed-rate conventional mortgage with a payment that's no more than 25 percent of your monthly take-home pay.
- **You're emotionally ready to sell.** Are you emotionally prepared to leave the place where your family made memories? Are you committed to keeping your home ready-for-show for weeks or even months? Are you ready to hear the harsh

reasons why potential buyers think your home isn't perfect? If the answer is no to any of those questions, now's not the time to sell.

- **Your home is worth more than you owe.** Selling a home that's worth less than you owe is a lousy deal. Breaking even on your home sale is better, but it's still not ideal. If you're in either situation, don't sell unless you need to avoid bankruptcy or foreclosure.

If all those describe you and you've found an excellent real estate agent you can trust, you're in great shape to sell your home.

Setting the Right Price

Once you've made the decision to sell, your next big decision is price. Your agent will walk you through their pricing strategy, but ultimately, the final number is up to you. As you work together to set your listing price, avoid these mistakes:

- **Mistake #1: Starting with sentiment.** How do you put a price on all those years of warm, fuzzy memories with your family? You don't. Buyers are no more attached to your place than any other home on the market. Price it too high and lots of buyers won't give it a second look.
- **Mistake #2: Using fuzzy math.** Don't base your sale price solely on how much money you need to get out of it. Focus on setting a price that makes sense in your market.

- **Mistake #3: Testing the market.** When the market's hot, it's tempting to see just how much you can get. After all, you can always drop the price if buyers don't bite. But that's a bad approach. Buyers don't waste time on overpriced homes, much less make offers on them. And the longer your listing stays on the market, the more people will assume there's something wrong with it.
- **Mistake #4: Trusting the internet.** In about 15 seconds you can get an estimated value of your home for free online. Check another site—get another value. That's interesting if you're just curious. But it's a problem if you're seriously trying to set a price for your home. This job calls for a real, live expert with personal experience in your market.

Get a Comparative Market Analysis

In the end, your home is worth what someone is willing to pay for it. The best way to get an idea about that number is to compare recent sales of homes like yours in your area. Your real estate agent will pull all that information into a comparative market analysis (CMA, or a comp), a detailed report that compares your home to nearby homes that are on the market or were recently sold. The goal is to find homes that are the most like yours and use their sale prices to set a competitive price for your home in your market.

Preparing Your Home for the Market

Today's buyers have high expectations about how a home should look. That means sellers have to work a lot harder to showcase their homes in just the right way for open houses and showings.

Staging is the art of highlighting the positives and downplaying the negatives in your home to give it a high-end feel. Good staging can help you sell your home faster, and some studies have even shown that staging can lead to higher offers. According to a recent NAR study, 81 percent of agents said staging made it easier for buyers to visualize a property as their future home.[4] And it makes sense, right? Who wants to buy a house that's in shambles and smells weird? If your house looks its absolute best, buyers will be motivated to make a competitive offer.

Home Staging Tips

Usually, there's no need to go overboard with your staging. But there are some basics you'll need to take care of no matter what:

- Scrub every surface until it shines.
- Minimize clutter to maximize space.
- Pay a pro to deep clean rugs and carpets.

---

4. National Association of REALTORS®, "Profile of Home Staging," nar. realtor (March 30, 2023), https://www.nar.realtor/research-and-statistics/ research-reports/profile-of-home-staging/.

- Paint walls in neutral colors to appeal to the most buyers and make rooms look their best.
- Don't forget curb appeal. The outside of your house needs to be as neat and inviting as the inside.

When you're ready to step up your staging, focus your efforts and your budget on the living room, primary bedroom and bath, and the kitchen and dining room. Here are some ideas for each area based on how much you have to spend:

Zero-Budget Ideas

- **Living room:** Arrange seating with conversation—not channel surfing—in mind. Borrow pieces from other rooms if needed.
- **Primary bedroom and bath:** Go minimal by storing bulky furniture. (That means you, treadmill!) In the bathroom, straighten up your linen closet and hide the hamper. Show off the space in your closets by cleaning out what you don't need, then packing it up and storing it.
- **Kitchen and dining room:** Clear off the countertops. Set the table with your best dishes, flatware, and linens.

Small-Budget Ideas

- **Living room:** Add fresh flowers to your mantle or coffee table. Update lighting fixtures. Buy new throw pillows for your sofa.

- **Primary bedroom and bath:** Create a spa-like feel with fresh, new bedding and throw pillows. Showcase the bathroom with new towels, and update the faucets and cabinet hardware.
- **Kitchen and dining room:** Refresh cabinets with new paint and hardware. Install an inexpensive backsplash. Refurbish or replace outdated light fixtures.
- **All rooms:** Well-lit rooms look larger, so put maximum-wattage light bulbs in *every* light in every room.

Large-Budget Ideas

- **Living room:** Bring worn-out flooring up to standard with the rest of the neighborhood. Replace shabby furniture or freshen it up with a new slipcover.
- **Primary bedroom and bath:** Add window treatments. Hire a pro to organize your closet. Upgrade the bathroom with granite countertops and ceramic-tile flooring.
- **Kitchen and dining room:** Upgrade to stainless appliances and natural-stone countertops. Install a higher-end light fixture over your dining table.

Go Pro for Your Photo Shoot

Once your home is looking its best, it's time for a photo shoot. Your listing photos are a big deal since most buyers start their home search online. In other words, this is not a job for the camera on your phone.

Your agent should have a good photographer on speed dial so that you don't have to round one up. All you need to do is add the final touches and get out of the way.

Get a Pre-Listing Home Inspection

The way your home looks will help get buyers in the door. But that doesn't mean you can ignore the nuts and bolts when you're getting ready to sell. A pre-listing home inspection will turn up any issues with the important systems before you put your home on the market. The inspection usually includes:

- Electrical, plumbing, and heating and cooling systems
- Walls, ceilings, floors, windows, and doors
- Roof, attic, and visible insulation
- Foundation, basement, and structural components

A qualified home inspector will examine every access point of your home to see if there are any health or safety issues. They'll give you a detailed report outlining what works, what doesn't, and recommendations for maintenance and repair. Don't worry about checking every single to-do off your list, but do pay attention to the big-ticket issues.

Your agent can help you sort through the findings, though the roof, electrical, plumbing, and HVAC systems take priority. If you have room in your budget, take care of those before planting the For Sale sign in your yard.

Home Showings

You've already put in a lot of work to get your home ready for the market. But this might be the toughest part—home showings. You have to keep your home looking sharp, even during the busyness of your day-to-day. This phase will go more smoothly if you get the whole family on board and start treating your home like it already belongs to someone else.

- **Make a daily to-do list.** Get in the habit of putting things away as soon as you're done with them, and work through a checklist of simple tasks to knock out before you leave every morning. That way, you're always ready for guests.

- **Pack up the pets.** Take the dogs or cats for a joyride or send them to Grandma's house so buyers can focus on your home's best features.

- **Give buyers some space.** Don't make things awkward by sticking around during a showing. Get out of the house so buyers can ask their questions and fall in love with your home on their own.

- **Tackle the toys.** Keep the kids' clutter to a minimum by storing most of it and keeping a few favorites for them to play with.

- **Enlist help from the kids.** Give Junior a job to do! You can make it fun with timed practice drills. And don't forget to recognize a job well done.

- **Provide important info.** Leave a copy of your home inspection report, a history of your utility bills, and a list of recent upgrades and improvements on the kitchen counter for prospective buyers.

You'll have days when you just can't get everything put away and make it out the door on time. Just let your agent know so they can prepare the buyer ahead of time. Don't miss an opportunity to get your home seen!

Showing an Empty Home

If you've already moved out, keeping your home show-ready is easier. You'll still want to stage the important spaces to give it that high-end feel and bring some life to the space. It also helps potential buyers envision living there.

Just don't forget about routine upkeep. Nothing's worse than a home that screams "Nobody lives here!" because the grass is knee-high and there's dust everywhere. Make plans to take care of those items or hire lawn and cleaning services to take care of them for you.

Choose the Right Offer

Showings naturally lead to offers. And offers have a lot of moving parts. Specifically, you'll want to pay attention to the closing date, purchase price, and contingencies. We'll walk through what to look for with these in general. But you can also rely on your agent to explain the terms of any offer you get so you can make the call on what to do next.

Closing Date

It takes time to close on a home purchase, usually 30–60 days. Cash offers can close faster than that. Just be sure the closing date on a buyer's offer doesn't put you in a bind to move out faster than you planned or drag things out so you're waiting forever to get your money.

Purchase Price

Unless you're in a super-competitive market, you'll likely get offers for less than your asking price. It's important to look beyond that and take the whole offer into account. Sometimes a lower offer might turn out to be an overall better deal.

Let's say a buyer offers you your full asking price of $250,000. But they want you to pay all their closing costs and throw in your washer and dryer. All that would cost you $10,000, netting you $240,000 from the deal (minus all your other costs like commission, closing costs, etc.).

Meanwhile, a second buyer offers $5,000 under your asking price without making any other special requests. You'd end up with $245,000 (minus other costs). You obviously walk away with more money with this deal.

Think of it this way: Even a low offer is an opportunity to get your home sold, so don't take it personally. With some skillful nego-tiating, you can turn a disappointing offer into a deal where both sides win.

And whatever you do, be sure to read the contracts thoroughly. You don't want to accidentally agree to sell your brand-new washing machine and dryer with your house.

Don't forget you also have a real estate agent on your side who does these kinds of deals every day. Your agent will have a good read on whether a potential buyer could get you tangled up in contingencies or give you a smooth path toward closing. So, trust your agent's experience and negotiation skills.

Contingencies

Contingencies are things that need to happen before your home sale can be finalized, like the sale of the buyer's home or the results of a home inspection. If those contingencies aren't met—the buyer's home doesn't sell in a certain time frame, for example, or the home inspection turns up big problems—the buyer or the seller can back out of the agreement. Contingencies aren't bad. But don't agree to any you're not comfortable with.

As the seller, you'll mainly want to pay attention to contingencies related to the home inspection, the appraisal, and the buyer's financing. Let's dig into each of these.

Home Inspection

Even if you paid for an inspection before you listed your home, your buyer will likely want to get an inspection of their own. Ideally, there won't be any big surprises. But don't panic if the buyer's home inspector uncovers a few issues yours didn't.

If new issues do pop up, your real estate agent can help you make the call on what needs to be fixed so you can close the deal. In some cases, you can offer cash at closing or a discount on the sales price to cover the cost of repairs. In other cases, the buyer's lender may require certain repairs before they'll approve the mortgage.

If you're dealing with a major fix, your agent can help you gather a few professional quotes for the repair. That way you have an accurate dollar amount to work with as you negotiate a solution that makes everybody happy.

Appraisal

At this stage in the game, the whole deal comes down to the appraisal. If your home appraises for less than the buyer has offered to pay, the lender won't approve the mortgage. That's why one of the first steps is to price your home according to the market. But it's also important to make sure the appraisal accurately represents your home. Here's how to improve your appraisal odds:

- Leave your home sparkling clean so the appraiser knows your home has been well maintained.
- Give the appraiser a detailed list of any improvements you've made to the home, and try to include invoices or receipts.
- Ask your agent to provide a well-researched list of houses similar to yours to support your sales price.

Financing

How do you keep lack of financing from killing your deal? When a buyer makes an offer, check to see if they've included a preapproval letter from a mortgage lender. If they have one, great! The lender has verified exactly how much they're willing to loan them.

Just know it's not bulletproof. Buyers lose jobs, open credit cards, and take out new car loans—any of which can throw a wrench into the final approval. If that happens, an experienced agent will help you make the best of a bad situation.

Once you've accepted the offer, though, the ball truly is in the buyer's court while you wait for the lender to approve their mortgage. But your agent will still be busy behind the scenes:

- Maintaining a stream of clear communication.
- Contacting the buyer's lender to push the approval process through on time.
- Actively investigating red flags that could put your deal in danger.
- Preparing to connect the buyer with an alternate lender if the original one falls through.

Handling Last-Minute Deal Breakers

Home deals go bad for lots of reasons. Here are some of the most common—and how you can deal with them.

- **A title search uncovers an open lien on your property.** Open liens (and any other title issues that give someone else the right to take possession of your house) must be cleared before you can close the deal. If the lien is covered under your title insurance policy, that should make it go away. If not, you'll have to resolve or pay the lien before you can close.
- **The home inspection identifies a big-ticket repair.** This means another round of negotiations with the buyer—and the potential for more money out of your pocket. Having an expert negotiator in your corner increases your chances of keeping the deal moving forward.
- **Your buyer's financing falls through.** Without financing, your buyer likely won't have the cash to close on the home. Unless your buyer secures another lender before closing day, you can pretty much count on going back to square one to find another buyer. Again, look for a buyer who is already preapproved—or paying in cash!
- **An issue comes up in the final walk-through.** Last-minute surprises in your home's condition must be handled before closing. Follow the Golden Rule by leaving the home the way you'd want someone to leave it for you.
- **Your home appraises for less than the sale price.** In this case, you could dispute a questionable appraisal. Otherwise, for the deal to go through, someone has to shell out more money to bridge the gap. Odds of recovery depend on how big the gap is between the appraisal value and the sales price.

You and the buyer may have to split the difference. Or you could lower your asking price.

Blast the Confetti—You Sold a House!

After you and the buyer sign the final paperwork and make your payments on closing day, you'll get your big, whopping check! And then that's it—you're done. You've sold your home the Ramsey way and set yourself up to keep building wealth that'll help you leave a legacy.

Investing in Real Estate

If all you ever do is buy and sell the homes you live in the way we just talked about—the Ramsey way—you'll build plenty of wealth. In fact, a paid-for home makes up a big chunk of most millionaires' net worth. In addition to that and my mutual-fund investments, I also love investing in paid-for real estate. Mark Twain got it right when he said, "Buy land. They're not making it anymore."

Generally speaking, real estate provides a better rate of return than mutual funds. But there's a bigger hassle factor, especially for rentals. So real estate investing isn't for everyone. And I'd never recommend it to anyone who isn't already on Baby Step 7 and maxing out their retirement accounts.

I know most of the advice and how-to's out there tell you to "leverage" debt to invest in real estate. If that's the kind of investing plan you're looking for, you're not going to get it here. Remember,

I'm the guy who got in debt up to my eyeballs to accumulate millions of dollars' worth of real estate, and I lost it all. I went bankrupt.

That experience broke me. But it also gave me the lesson I needed: to quit borrowing money. From that point on, I only purchased properties with 100 percent cash. And now I own several hundred million dollars' worth of real estate. I don't owe a dime to anyone for any of it . . . and I never will.

I'm reminding you of this because I know from my own experience that you don't have to use debt to "make it" as a real estate investor. Investing in real estate the Ramsey way involves zero debt—but a lot of hard work and patience. Because the best way to get rich quick is to get rich slow. Find good deals, pay for them in cash, and in the long run, your investment properties will stack money for you and build wealth for your legacy.

Types of Real Estate Investments

Let's talk through the most common types of real estate investing.

Homeownership

Our culture needs a mindset shift. Everyone wants to buy a home, but you need to be focused on *owning* the place. Like I mentioned before, homeownership is the first step in real estate investing—and a huge step toward financial peace. A paid-for home means security, a huge boost to your net worth, and more money to put toward wealth-building. Imagine what you could do if you didn't have a house payment every month! With no debt and no mortgage payment, how much faster could you reach your goal of investing in paid-for real estate? See what I mean? This stuff really works!

Bottom line: Pay off the house you live in before investing in any other real estate.

Rental Properties

You'll often hear people say rental properties are a way to generate passive income. The idea is, you don't have to put in a lot of work to get the benefit. Here's the truth: Rental properties are anything but passive. Finding and buying the property is just the first step. After that, you have to find renters and take care of repairs and maintenance. Whether you do them yourself or hire a property management company, those responsibilities are on you for as long as you own the property.

Being a landlord has other challenges. They're called renters. The best way to deal with problem renters is to avoid them by doing your homework. Ask for references from their previous landlords to make sure they pay their rent and will treat your place with respect. And always have your renters sign a written lease. That way, everyone on both sides of the agreement understands what's expected. If there's a disagreement—everything's on paper.

Get a contract lawyer to review your lease to make sure it covers all the bases. Plus, if you ever need to evict a tenant who's causing trouble or missing rent, you'll already have an attorney.

I don't say all that to discourage you from investing in rentals. I have plenty of them myself. But you do need to know what you're getting into. All that work can pay off big in a few different ways.

- Increase in property value: If you ever sell, you'll turn a nice profit.
- Cash flow: Rental income can add thousands of dollars to your annual income. Just be prepared for seasons when you don't have renters.
- Depreciation: Talk to your tax advisor about tax breaks for your rental properties.

Speaking of taxes, real estate taxes can get tricky fast, so do yourself a favor and work with a tax professional. Meet with them regularly to discuss your investments and how they impact your taxes—you don't want to get slapped with a penalty! If you don't already have a tax expert you trust, you can use the QR code to find a RamseyTrusted tax pro.

House Flipping

If you do it right, you can see a return on your real estate investment faster by flipping a house than renting it. That means you buy it, make your improvements, and sell it—all within a few weeks or months.

When I did my first house flip, I only turned an $800 profit. (Yeah. Pretty lame.) And I only made that much because I crawled around under the house doing the pipework myself! Plus, it took 90 days to sell the stinkin' thing!

Looking back, I can see I paid too much for the property. I was 21 years old and way too excited to be a real estate investor. That's a mistake most beginners make. There's just something about real estate that gets our emotions out of whack. They take over and we end up making bad decisions—like overpaying. You've got to think of your real estate investment as a mathematical transaction and nothing else. Because with house flipping, the deal is made at the buy. You've got to get a great deal on the front end to make a decent profit once all is said and done.

I always try to buy property at 70 percent of value minus repairs. That's the kind of discount you're looking for when you're flipping houses. And that's going to take patience. If the price isn't right, wait. Another opportunity will come along.

You also need to be realistic about the amount of work you'll have to do. Flipping houses isn't as glamorous (or as fast or easy) as TV shows make it seem. If you love hands-on work, have at it! If you don't, you'd better hire a contractor. And either way, budget plenty of time and money to get the work done. Renovations almost always cost more and take longer than you think they will, especially when you hire a contractor.

And, just like any other investment, there's a risk you could lose money—if the market changes, you overpay, or the house turns out to be a dud. Before you jump in headfirst, talk to a real estate agent about the potential in your market for successful house flipping.

Six Principles for Investing in Real Estate

Alright, now let's talk strategy. Here are six principles for you to stick to when you're ready to invest in real estate beyond your primary home.

1: Pay in Cash

Yep, I'm going to keep repeating this until it sticks. It's the most important piece of advice I can give you. Always pay for investment properties in cash—in full—and that goes for any updates or renovations too. Don't even think about going into debt for this!

Debt always equals risk—and the riskier your investment, the more likely you are to lose everything. Trust me, I've done detailed research, and 100 percent of foreclosures occur on a home with a mortgage.

I'm okay with people having mortgage debt on their personal home because it's an appreciating asset (and you're going to pay that loan off early!). I'm not okay with you getting a mortgage (and especially a second mortgage if you haven't paid off your house) to buy an investment property.

A 100 percent down payment takes debt out of the equation and lowers your risk. Can't find a tenant for your rental property? Who cares—without a mortgage, you don't need renters right away. Housing market took a nosedive right when you wanted to sell the house you flipped? That's okay. You can afford to wait for the market to pick back up.

Paying in full also sets you up to make money sooner. Instead of repaying a lender, you get to keep all the profits. That's how to invest in real estate wisely!

Now, this means you won't be able to invest in real estate with just a little money. And that's okay. If all you've got is a little money, put it toward your retirement—which brings us to the next principle.

2: Diversify

Remember Baby Step 4? That's when you invest 15 percent of your household income into retirement accounts. You'll invest in good growth stock mutual funds inside those accounts, and that will be the foundation of your wealth-building strategy. After that's locked and loaded, and you've reached Baby Step 7, you can start investing in paid-for real estate. (See page x for the complete list of Baby Steps if you need a refresher.)

Oh, and don't cash out your retirement savings to buy property—or anything else. Your real estate investing funds should be separate from your retirement savings.

3: Stay Local

Don't buy an investment property in Arizona if you live in Illinois! When you live far away from your properties, you're forced to blindly trust a management company to handle your business—and that makes it much harder to hold them accountable.

Now, it might still be a good idea to hire a management group, even if you're local, to help things run smoothly. But you—and only you—are the property owner. So stay close and keep tabs on your investments.

4: Be Prepared for Risks

Like I talked about, renting out property isn't as simple as getting renters and checking in once a year. Even in the best situations, appliances break and roofs leak. Sometimes rentals sit empty for months if you can't find the right renter. And you might even lose rental income if you face an eviction moratorium like the one we saw during COVID-19, which temporarily banned evictions for non-payment of rent. The best way to prepare for risks like those and to cover unexpected expenses is by paying for everything with cash and having a fully funded emergency fund.

5: Start Small

Not sure real estate investing is for you? Test it. Try renting out a space above your garage or an extra bedroom—even for a few nights at a time. That'll give you a taste of what owning a rental is like.

Or, if you don't want to be a landlord, you could dip your toe into REITs (real estate investment trusts). REITs are like mutual funds, but they invest in real estate instead of stocks. Of all the options we've talked about, this is the most passive way to earn money from a real estate investment. Work with an investing advisor to choose a well-run REIT with a good track record of returns similar to a good growth stock mutual fund (10–12 percent average annual returns). And limit your REIT investment to no more than 10 percent of your net worth.

It's also wise to talk to other real estate investors. Get lunch with them and ask them what they wish they'd known before getting started.

6: Hire a Real Estate Agent

I can't stress this enough: You need a local real estate agent who's been doing this for years. They'll know what areas of town you should look into and what hurdles you might face as a real estate investor. And when it's time to buy a property, they can help you get a better deal than you'd get on your own.

Why Pay Off Your Own Home First?

I get it—if you've got to wait until your home is paid for before you can invest in real estate, you might feel like you'll never get to do it. And if opportunity is knocking at your door right now, the thought of missing out is eating you up inside. But trust me on this. It's worth it to wait until you're really ready.

Let's say you owe $150,000 on your house. You've got a 15-year fixed-rate mortgage at 2.5 percent interest, and you're paying $1,360 a month on it. We'll also say you're bringing home $5,500 per month—so your mortgage payment is a little less than 25 percent of your monthly take-home pay. Way to go!

You come across a can't-pass-it-up deal on a rental property for $150,000, and you're convinced the extra income will help you move through your goals faster. So you use the $30,000 you have in savings as a down payment, and you take out a 15-year fixed-rate mortgage to buy the rental.

Interest rates are a lot higher now than when you bought your home, and they're even higher for investment properties. That means the payment on your rental property also clocks in at about $1,360. But you're not worried, because you plan to rent out the house for $1,500 a month. That'll more than cover the mortgage on the rental.

I've got news for you. Anyone who thinks the rent will cover the mortgage payment has never owned rental property before.

What you couldn't foresee is that it'll take three months to find renters. Which means you'll pay over $4,000 in mortgage payments on your rental while it sits empty. Between that and the payment on your home, you'll spend almost half your income on mortgage payments during that time!

You're going to feel like you can barely breathe. What will you do if the air-conditioning unit goes out or the dishwasher starts leaking? What if your kid gets sick? What if you lose your job?

That's why you don't rush it. Real estate can be a fantastic investment—if you do it the right way. Be smart. Pay off your own house, invest in your retirement accounts, and save, save, save so you can pay in full for your investment properties. Set yourself up for success, not struggle.

Build Your Real Estate Legacy

I hope you see now what I mean by making homeownership a blessing, not a burden. I hope you feel like you know exactly how to make that happen for your family. I hope you're pumped about actually owning a paid-for house and never owing a penny to anyone ever again.

The Ramsey way of doing real estate is about more than the nuts and bolts of the how-to. It's about the resounding victory cry I hear in the voices of a husband and wife visiting my radio studio with locked hands, grinning ear-to-ear to tell me they're 100 percent debt-free—the house and everything!

That's the kind of stuff that puts your heart in your throat and brings tears to your eyes. It's the kind of thing we're all longing for. A sense of home. A sense of peace. A place we can go to take refuge when the world chews us up and spits us out. A place to rest, heal, and regroup.

I want that for you. I want your home to be a sanctuary. I want your house to build outrageous wealth for you. Wealth that leaves a legacy for your kids, your grandkids, and their grandkids. That's my hope and prayer for you in writing this little book.

All you need to do is follow the plan. Now get out there and have some fun with real estate. We'll always be here, cheering you on. And if you ever need help along the way, give us a call.

I can't wait to hear your real estate story.

Did this book positively impact your life?

If so, it would be a huge help to me if you post about it on social media using #theramseyway. This is how we get the word out to help more people.